# 51 things to make with Cardboard Tubes

**Fiona Hayes**

QEB

# Contents

## Basic Equipment

Most of these projects use some or all of the following equipment, so keep these handy:

- **White glue**
- **Scissors**
- **Pencils**
- **Ruler**
- **Felt-tip pens**
- **Paintbrushes**
- **Clothespins**

# Giraffe

This cute giraffe will turn your bedroom into a safari wonderland! You could even make a herd of them!

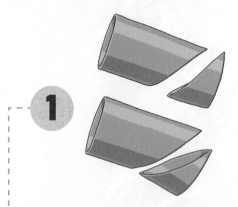

**1** Cut the corner off two short tubes and one long tube.

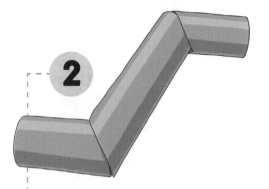

**2** Glue the tubes together, as shown. They should slide into each other a bit.

**3** Cut the corner off another two short tubes to make the legs. Glue the legs to the body.

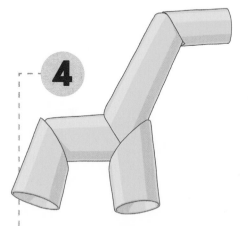

**4** Paint the tubes yellow, then when completely dry, add some brown spots.

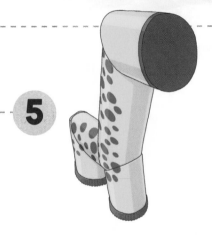

**5**

Glue a circle of brown corrugated cardstock to the front of the head, and some thin strips of it to the bottom of the legs, for hooves.

**6**

Glue a narrow strip of brown corrugated cardstock along the back of the neck, for the mane. Cut some ears and two short sections off the straw for the horns. Glue in place.

**7**

Add a smile. To make the eyes stand out, add colored felt circles before you stick on the eyes. Your giraffe is ready!

**Handy Hint**
Slightly flatten the short tubes to make them easier to cut.

5

# Lovely Lion

ROAAAR! Who's the king of the jungle? This gorgeous yellow lion! Put it at the foot of your bed to guard all your toys.

## You will need

**Five short tubes**
**Cardboard**
**Yellow paint**
**Brown cardstock**
**Two googly eyes**
**One black pompom**

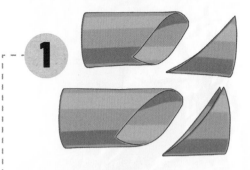

**1** Cut the corner off one end of two short tubes.

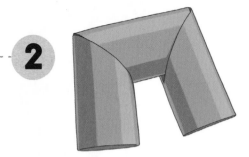

**2** To make the body, glue the tubes to either end of another tube, as shown. They should slide into each other a bit.

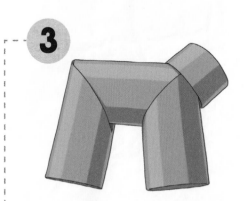

**3** Cut a ring from another tube. Glue it to the body, to make the neck.

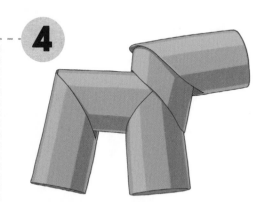

**4** Cut the corner off the last tube and glue it to the neck. This is the head. Add a circle of cardboard to the end of the head. Paint the lion yellow.

**5**

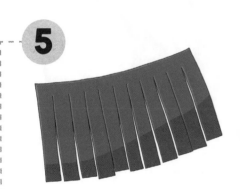

Cut slits along a strip of brown cardstock. This will be the mane.

**6**

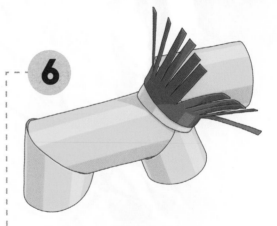

Glue the cardstock in place. You may need two strips to make a really thick mane.

**7**

Add some googly eyes, a pompom nose, and a smile! Can you hear the lion roar?

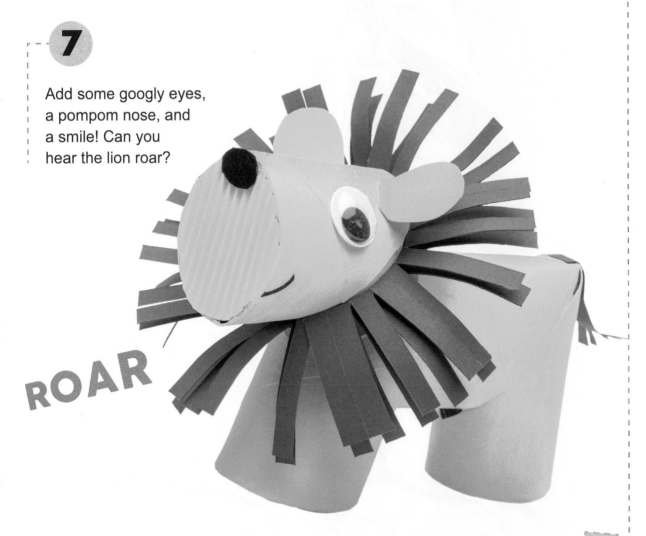

ROAR

# Birdhouse

## You will need

One short tube

Cardstock

Paint

String

One straw

**1**

Paint a short tube any color you choose.

**2**

To make the roof, cut a semi-circle from cardstock. Glue a piece of string in the middle, as shown.

**3**

Roll the semi-circle into a cone and glue the edges together. Make sure the string extends from the pointed end. Hold in place with a clothespin and leave to dry.

**4**

Cut out a doorway. Use a pencil to make the hole under the doorway.

**5**

Glue the roof to the base.

**6**

For the perch, glue on a short length of straw. Why not make a few houses and hang them up together?

# Bouncy Bunny

**1**

Cut two narrow rings from a short tube. These will be the ears.

**2**

Paint another short tube and the ears brown.

**3**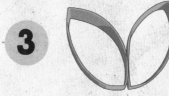

Press the ears together and glue in shape.

**4**

Glue the ears onto the top of the other tube.

**5**

Cut out a circle of felt, for the belly. Glue in place.

**6**

Add a nose, googly eyes, and a happy smile. Use different colored paint to make some friends for your rabbit.

9

# Chickens

Cluck, cluck, cluck! These pretty, spotted chickens will brighten up any room. You could make a set and line them up on a shelf.

## You will need

Two short tubes
Paint
Red felt or cardstock
Yellow cardstock
Four googly eyes

**1**

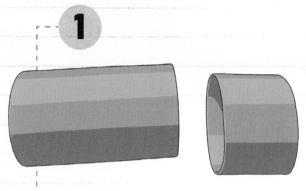

For each chicken, cut a short tube, as shown. Use the longer pieces for your chickens and recycle the rest.

**2**

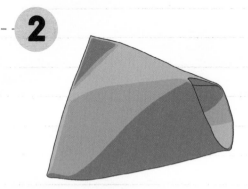

Flatten one end of each tube and glue it together.

**3**

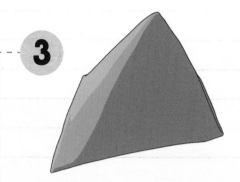

Flatten the other end of each tube the opposite way to step 2, and glue it together. Paint your chickens.

**4**

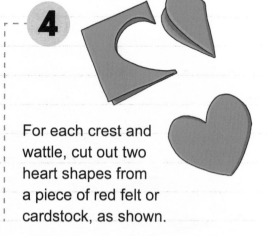

For each crest and wattle, cut out two heart shapes from a piece of red felt or cardstock, as shown.

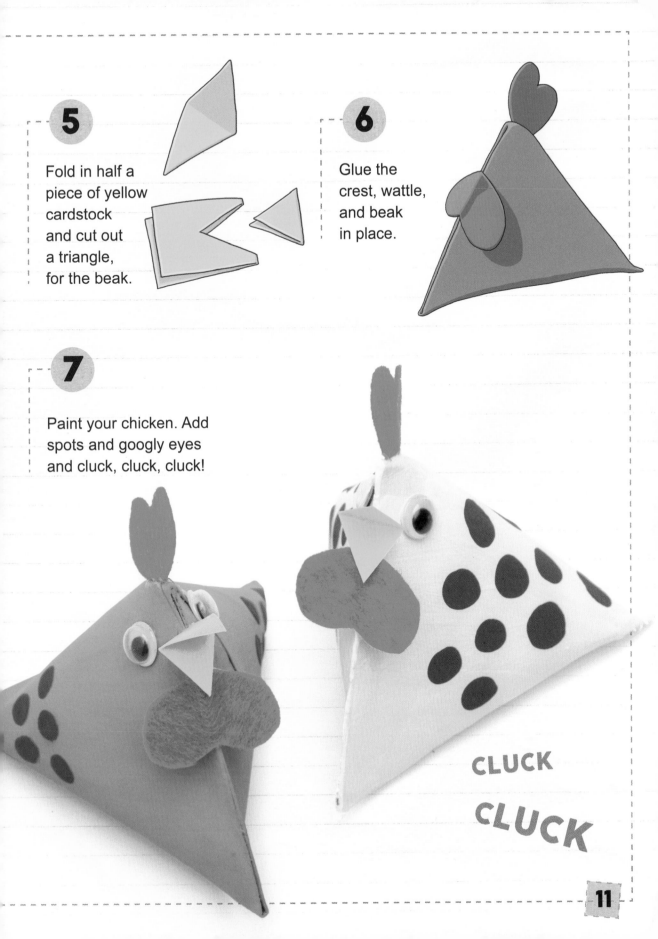

**5**

Fold in half a piece of yellow cardstock and cut out a triangle, for the beak.

**6**

Glue the crest, wattle, and beak in place.

**7**

Paint your chicken. Add spots and googly eyes and cluck, cluck, cluck!

CLUCK

CLUCK

# Daisies

Do you love flowers? If you do, you will adore these beautiful daisies. Make a bunch of them and put them in a vase.

**1**

To make one flower, paint two short tubes on the inside and outside.

**2**

Put a rubber band around the top of each tube, as shown. Cut slits up to the band.

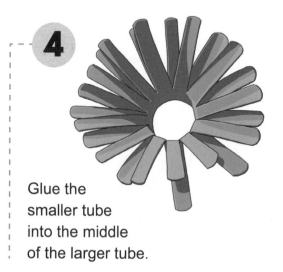

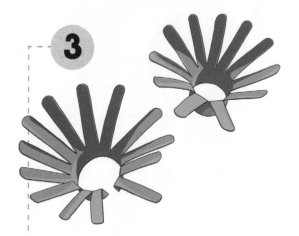

**3**

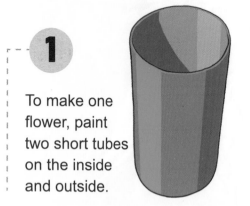

Bend the pieces outward, to make petals. Cut one of the tubes, to make the diameter slightly smaller, and re-glue.

**4**

Glue the smaller tube into the middle of the larger tube.

**5**

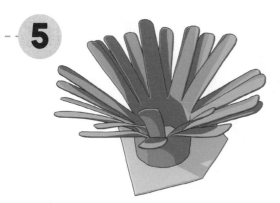

Glue the back of the daisy to a piece of cardboard. When dry, cut away the excess cardboard and paint it green.

**6**

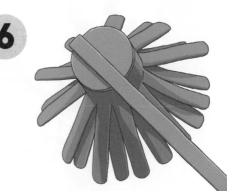

Glue a narrow strip of cardboard to the back of the daisy for the stem. Paint it green.

**7**

Scrunch up some tissue paper and glue it into the middle of the flower to finish off the pretty bloom.

# Dragonfly

What is pretty, brightly colored, and flits around a garden pond? A beautiful dragonfly! Make this cute little friend, or two or three!

## You will need

One short tube
One long tube
Paint
Bubble wrap
Felt
Two googly eyes

**1**

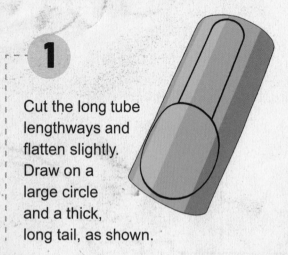

Cut the long tube lengthways and flatten slightly. Draw on a large circle and a thick, long tail, as shown.

**2**

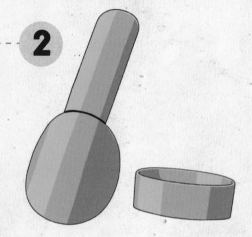

Cut out the shape. Cut a narrow ring from the short tube.

**3**

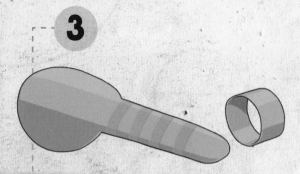

Paint on your design—stripes or spots will look good. Don't forget to paint the narrow ring too. Leave to dry.

**4**

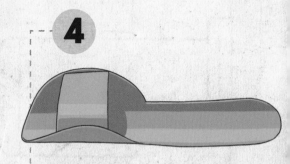

Glue the narrow ring underneath your dragonfly's body. Use clothespins to hold it in place until dry.

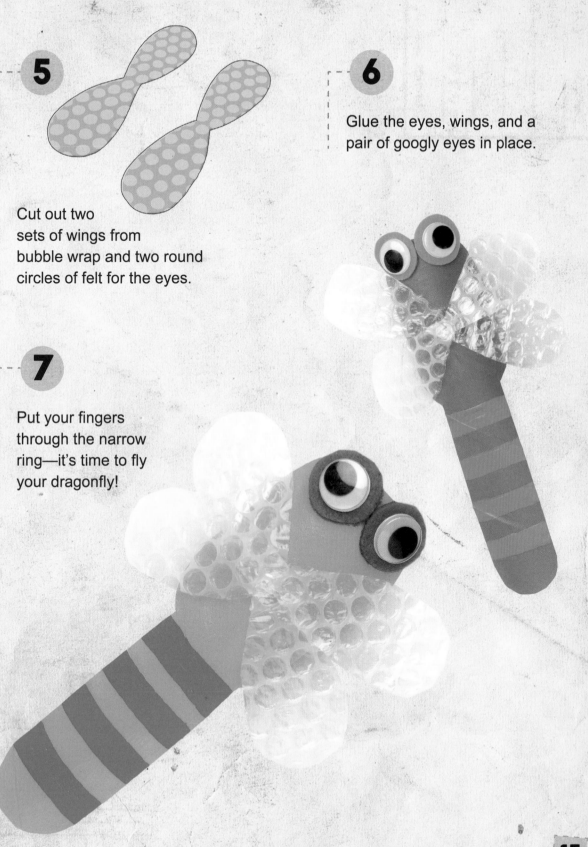

**5**

Cut out two sets of wings from bubble wrap and two round circles of felt for the eyes.

**6**

Glue the eyes, wings, and a pair of googly eyes in place.

**7**

Put your fingers through the narrow ring—it's time to fly your dragonfly!

15

# Cute Duck

Quack, quack, quack!
This gorgeous little duck
is lots of fun to make and
even more fun to play with!

## You will need

**Three short tubes**

**Yellow and
orange paint**

**Cardboard**

**Googly eyes**

**1**

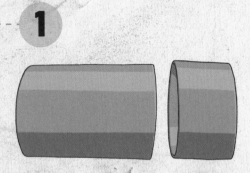

Cut a short tube, as shown. Keep
the larger section for the duck's
legs, recycle the smaller piece.

**2**

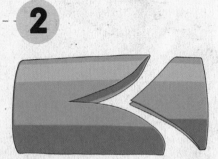

To make the head, cut out a
long, curved V from one end
of another tube.

**3**

Cut a large oval from another
short tube. Glue the legs to the
underside. Hold in place with
clothespins until dry.

**4**

Glue the head to the
top of the body.

**5**

Cut out a pair of webbed feet from the cardboard and paint them orange.

**6**

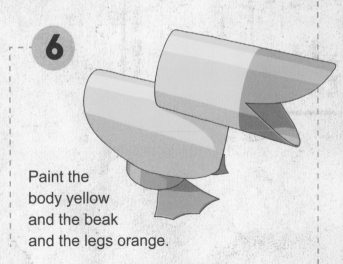

Paint the body yellow and the beak and the legs orange.

QUACK
QUACK

**7**

Add some googly eyes to finish off this cute and colorful duck!

# Cake and Candles

## You will need

**At least 12 short tubes**

**Paint, including white and brown**

**Yellow and white cardstock**

**Cardboard**

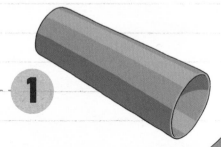

**1**

For each candle, cut a small strip of cardboard the same width as a short tube. Glue this strip into one end of the tube.

**2**

Paint the candle. Cut out a flame shape from yellow cardstock. Glue it to the strip in the middle of the candle.

**3**

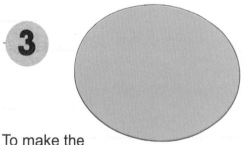

To make the cake, cut out two large circles from cardboard.

**4**

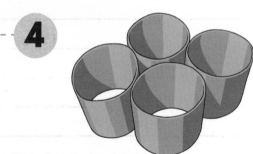

Cut about six short tubes in half, to make 12 halves.

**5**

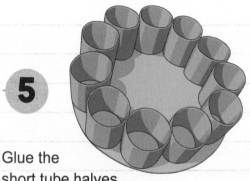

Glue the short tube halves around the inside edge of one of the circles.

**6**

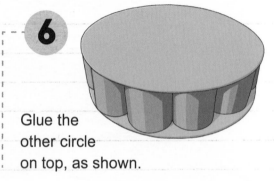

Glue the other circle on top, as shown.

**7**

Cut a strip of white cardstock. Keep one edge straight but make the other wobbly. This will be the cake icing.

**8**

Glue the icing around the top edge of the cake. Paint the top white and the rest of the cake a chocolate-brown.

**9**

Glue the candles in place. Your birthday cake is ready...Happy birthday to you!

**Handy Hint**

Use a piece of cardstock as a spatula to spread glue.

# Super Specs

If you love glasses and fun accessories, you will love these wild and wacky specs!

**1**

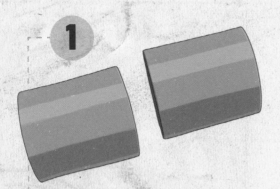

Cut a short tube in half. Paint both pieces—use a different color on the insides.

**2**

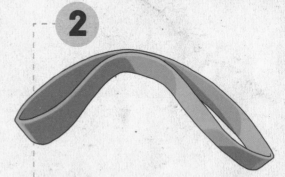

Cut a narrow section from another short tube and paint it the same color as the outside of the tubes. Bend it a little.

**3**

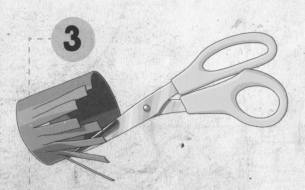

Cut slits along one edge of each short tube half, as shown.

**4**

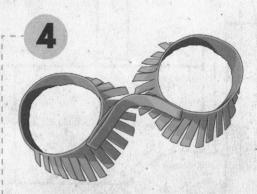

Glue the narrow section to the solid parts of the tubes.

**5**

Cut out two arms from cardboard, and paint.

**6**

Glue the arms to the outside edges of the tubes. Put on your glasses—how do you look?

TOO
COOL

# Pretty Fish

What's brightly colored, swims under the sea, and blows bubbles? This cute fish!

## You will need

One short tube
Paint
Cardboard
Two googly eyes

**1** Cut out a curved V from the end of a short tube.

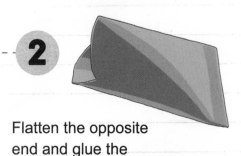

**2** Flatten the opposite end and glue the edges together.

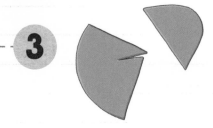

**3** Cut a fin and tail from cardboard. Cut a slit in the tail, so it will slide onto the end of the fish.

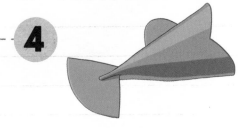

**4** Use a pencil to make a hole for your scissors on the top. Cut a slit on the top, for the fin to slide into. Glue the tail and fin in place.

**5** Paint the fish with spots or stripes. Add some googly eyes. Why not make a whole school of fish and hang them up?

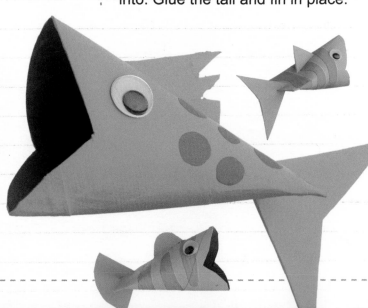

# Flowers

**Did you love making the daisies on page 12? Here are some more beautiful blooms to add to them.**

## You will need

**Five short tubes**
**Paint**
**Green paper**
**Yellow cardstock**

**1**

To make each flower, lightly compress a tube and draw five evenly spaced lines. Cut along the lines to make six rings.

**2**

Squeeze the rings so they look like petals.

**3**

Glue the rings together to make a flower, as shown. Hold in place with clothespins until dry. Paint your flower.

**4**

Make a stem for your flower by rolling a thin piece of green paper around a pencil. Start from the corner and roll diagonally until the end. Slide out the pencil before you glue the paper in place. Glue the stem to the middle of the flower.

**5**

Repeat steps 1 to 4 to make more flowers. Glue a circle of cardstock to the center of each flower. You can bend the stems to angle your flowers.

# Toothy Shark

Is it safe to go swimming today? Well, this smiling, speeding shark won't harm you! You could put it in your bathroom to scare your guests, though!

## You will need

**One long tube**
**Gray and white paint**
**Blue and white felt**
**Two googly eyes**

**1**

Slightly flatten a long tube so it is easier to cut. Cut out a V from one end. Keep this piece for the tail and fin.

**2**

Using a pencil, make a hole in the long piece of tube. Then cut a slot for the fin to slide into.

**3**

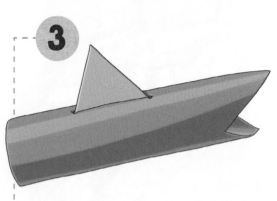

Glue the fin in place.

**4**

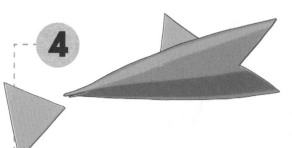

Flatten the uncut end of the tube, glue the edges together. Cut a slit in the tail and slide onto the back of the shark.

**5**

Paint the shark gray. Add some white gills. Cut out some blue felt circles and glue them on. Add the googly eyes, as shown.

**6**

Cut some narrow strips of white felt. Cut out little Vs along one edge, for the teeth.

**7**

Glue the teeth along the inside of the mouth to give your shark a toothy grin!

## Handy Hint

If you don't have a long tube, tape two short tubes together.

# Train

Make this multi-colored train—it will be the best on any track.

## You will need

Five short tubes

Cardboard

Tube cap

Paint

Ribbon

**1** Cut out a curved section from one end of a short tube.

**2** Glue the curved edge to the side of another tube.

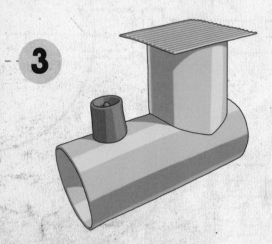

**3** Glue a square of cardboard to the top. Paint the train engine a pretty bright color. Add a tube cap for the funnel, as shown.

### Handy Hint

To make a circle, draw around a jar lid and cut out.

**4**

**5**

Paint three other tubes for the train cars. To make wheels, cut out four circles of cardboard for each car and six circles for the engine. Paint and glue them into position.

**6**

Make a long line of cars for the train to pull!

Cut some pieces of ribbon. Glue to the inside of the engine and cars, as shown.

CHOO **CHOO**

# Friendly Fox

**1** Fold the top of a short tube, as shown. Glue in place.

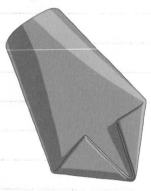

**2** Paint the top part of the tube brown and the underneath white. Paint on a black nose.

**3** Cut out two triangles from the cardstock, for ears. Paint them brown and glue them in place.

**4** Add two googly eyes, whiskers, and other details. Quick, hide the chickens!

# Frog

## You will need

One short tube
Green and yellow paint
Two googly eyes

**1**

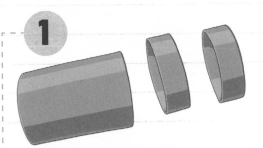

Cut two narrow rings from a short tube.

**2**

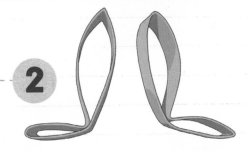

Flatten the rings and fold, as shown, to make the legs.

**3**

Glue the legs to the body.

**4**

Paint your frog green, with a yellow belly.

**5**

Add some eyes and a smile... Ribbit, ribbit, your frog is ready!

# Chinese Lanterns

## You will need

**One short tube**
**Paint**
**Cardstock**

**1**

Paint the inside and outside of a short tube and cut it along its length.

**2**

Flatten the tube and fold in half lengthways. Cut slits from the folded edge, as shown. Don't cut to the top!

**3**

Re-roll the tube and glue the edges together.

**4**

Lightly compress the tube, to make the slits fold out.

**5**

Cut a thin strip of cardstock for a handle and glue to the top of the lantern. Use clothespins to hold in place.

**6**

Your lantern is ready. Make lots more lanterns and hang them up with string.

# Totem Pole

**1**

Paint three short tubes different colours.

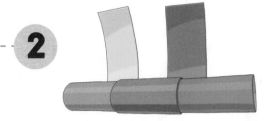

**2**

Cut and paint two strips of cardboard. Glue the cardboard around the tubes, making one long, sturdy tube.

**3**

Cut out a rectangle from cardboard. Cut a curved edge into one side of the rectangle, as shown. Paint. Cut two slits in the top of the first tube. Push the rectangle into the slits.

**4**

Cut a circle from the cardboard and paint it. Glue it over the top tube. Add felt circles, googly eyes, beaks, and scary mouths made from cardboard.

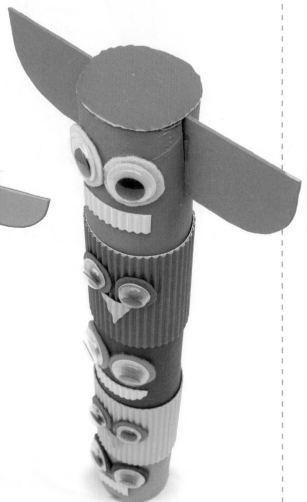

# Caterpillar

This cute and colorful caterpillar will brighten up any bedroom. Why not hang it from your ceiling?

## You will need

**Five short tubes**
**Paint, including red**
**Ribbon**
**One foam ball**
**Two googly eyes**
**Two bendy straws**

**1** Paint some short tubes different colors. When dry, cut the tubes into three sections.

**2** Place the cut tubes side by side—mix up the colors. Glue a long piece of ribbon to the top of each tube.

**3** Paint a tube red, and when dry, cut it into thin rings, as shown.

**4**

Glue the narrow red rings onto the ribbon. Turn over so the ribbon is on the bottom.

**5**

Paint a foam ball and glue it to the front of your caterpillar. Add some googly eyes.

**6**

Use a pencil to make two holes on the top of the ball. Insert two short straws and glue in place. Your creepy, crawly caterpillar is ready!

**Handy Hint**

Allow the glue to dry completely before moving your caterpillar.

# Awesome Owls

**1**

To make each owl, push in the sides of the top of a short tube, as shown, and paint it a bright color.

**2**

From felt, cut out two wings and an orange beak.

**3**

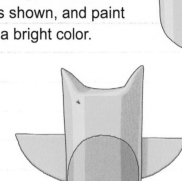

Cut a circle out of felt and glue it in place, as shown. Glue the wings in place.

**4**

Glue the beak in place. Cut out two circles of felt—they should be slightly larger than the eyes. Glue the eyes to the felt, then glue onto the owl. Cut a small slit into either side of your owl, so you can stand it on a tree branch. Repeat steps 1 to 4 to make two more owls.

**5**

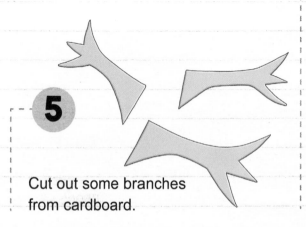

Cut out some branches from cardboard.

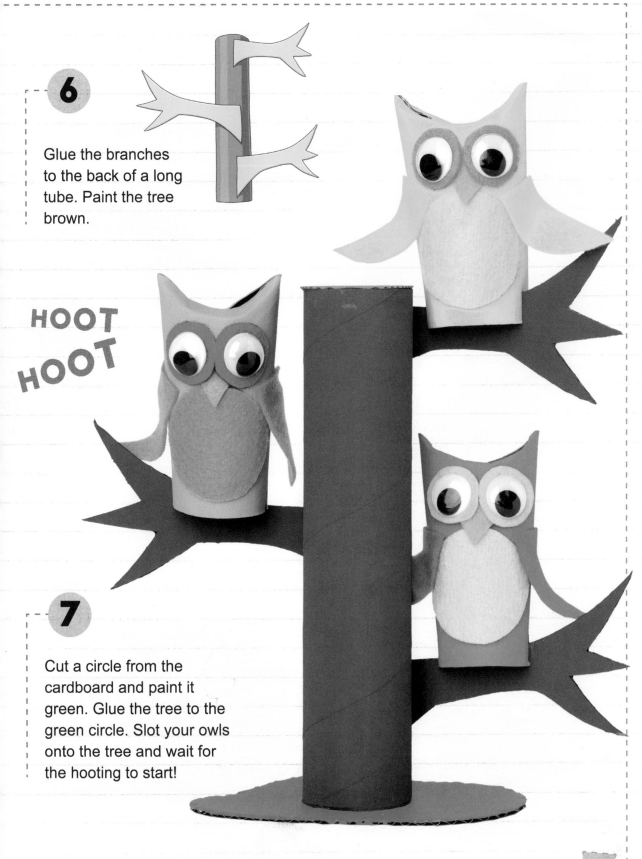

**6**

Glue the branches to the back of a long tube. Paint the tree brown.

HOOT
HOOT

**7**

Cut a circle from the cardboard and paint it green. Glue the tree to the green circle. Slot your owls onto the tree and wait for the hooting to start!

35

# Pencils

## You will need

**Four short tubes**
**Paint**
**Cardstock**

**1**

Paint a short tube. Glue the bottom to some cardstock.

**2**

When dry, cut away the excess cardstock.

**3**

Cut out a semi-circle from a piece of cardstock. Use scrapbooking scissors, if you have some, to cut along the curved edge.

**4**

Roll the cardstock into a cone and glue together. Hold in place with a clothespin until dry.

**5**

Paint the top of the cone the same color as the base. Repeat these steps to make a whole set of pencils. To make them different sizes, just cut pieces off the tubes before you start.

# Wiener Dog

## You will need

One short tube
One long tube
Paint, including black
Cardboard
Two googly eyes

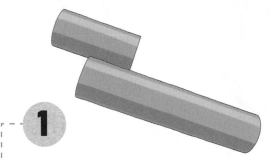

**1**

Glue a short tube to a long one, as shown.

**2**

Cut out four legs from cardboard, as shown.

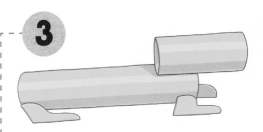

**3**

Glue the legs in place. Paint the dog.

**4**

Cut out two ears and a tail from cardboard. Paint them a contrasting color.

**5**

Glue the ears and tail in place. Cut out a small circle and paint it black, for the nose. Cut a small slit in the top of the head and slide the nose in place. Glue to hold in position. Add some googly eyes and a smile. Your little pooch is ready to play!

# Octopus

This amazing octopus looks so great that you'll feel you are exploring the deep for real!

## You will need

One short tube
Paint
Rubber band
Two googly eyes

**1**

Paint a short tube inside and out. Use a contrasting color on the inside.

**2**

Put a rubber band around the tube, as shown. Cut eight evenly spaced slits up to the band.

**3**

Remove the band and roll each section around a pencil.

**4**

Now your octopus has eight legs.

**5**

Paint on some spots and a smile, and add some googly eyes to this eight-legged sea creature.

# Tractor

## You will need

**Two short tubes**
**Paint**
**Cardboard**
**Blue cardstock**
**One tube cap**

**1**

Cut out a curved section from one end of a short tube.

**2**

Glue the curved edge to the side of another tube.

**3**

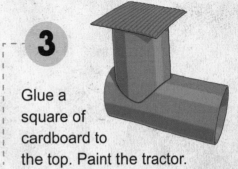

Glue a square of cardboard to the top. Paint the tractor.

**4**

For wheels, cut out two large and two small circles from cardboard, and paint them.

**5**

Glue the wheels to the sides of the tractor.

**6**

Add some cardstock rectangles for windows. Glue a tube cap to the front for the chimney.

# Mini Mice

Are you scared of mice? Well, there is nothing scary about these cuddly friends. You'll want to make lots and lots of them!

## You will need

**Two short tubes**

**Light gray, dark gray and pink paint**

**Pink felt**

**Four googly eyes**

**1**

Flatten one end of a short tube and glue the sides together.

**2**

Flatten the other end the opposite way to step 1, and glue the sides together. Repeat steps 1 and 2 with another short tube.

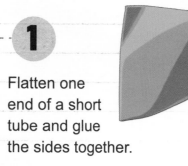

**3**

Paint the mice, as shown—don't forget the noses! Cut out some ears and a tail from pink felt, glue in place.

**4**

Glue on some googly eyes and wait for the happy squeaks to begin!

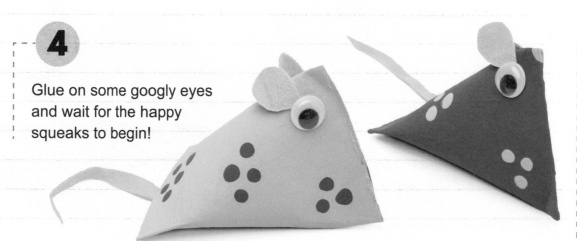

# Pink Piglet

**Snort, grunt, snort, grunt! It's piglet-making time—have fun!**

**1**

Push the sides of a short tube in, to create a curved top. Paint the tube pink.

**2**

Wrap a thin strip of pink cardstock around a pencil to curl it into a tail.

**3**

Cut out an oval of pink felt for the snout, paint on some nostrils, and glue it in place. Glue on the tail and some googly eyes with blue felt circles.

OINK OINK

# Red Squirrel

You have probably seen lots of gray squirrels, but red squirrels are far rarer—and very, very beautiful, just like this one!

**1**

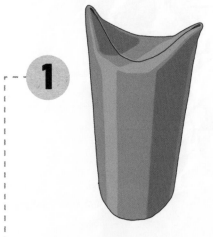

Push the sides of a short tube into the center, to create a curved top. Paint light brown.

**2**

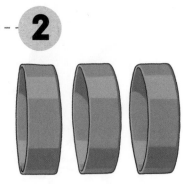

Cut three narrow rings from another short tube. Paint light brown.

**3**

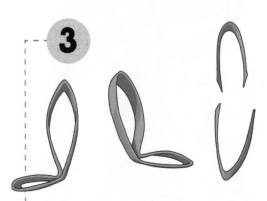

Bend two rings as shown, for the legs. Cut the last ring in half, for the arms.

**4**

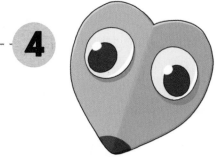

Cut out a heart shape from cardboard and lightly fold down the middle. Glue on some googly eyes and paint on a small nose.

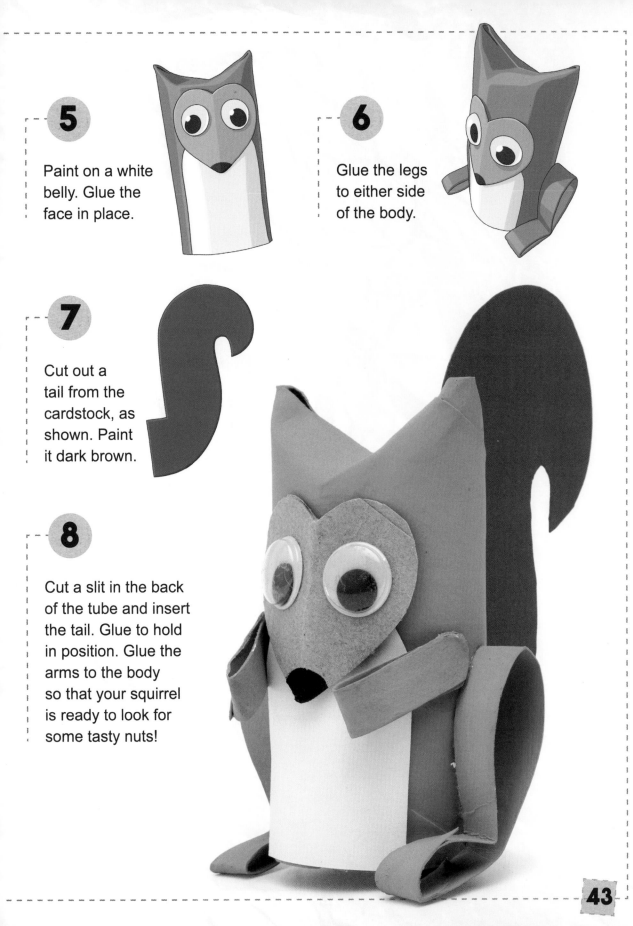

**5**

Paint on a white belly. Glue the face in place.

**6**

Glue the legs to either side of the body.

**7**

Cut out a tail from the cardstock, as shown. Paint it dark brown.

**8**

Cut a slit in the back of the tube and insert the tail. Glue to hold in position. Glue the arms to the body so that your squirrel is ready to look for some tasty nuts!

# Robin Finger Puppet

**You will need**

Two short tubes

Brown and black paint

Four googly eyes

Red, brown, yellow, white, and green felt

**1**

Flatten one end of a short tube and glue the sides together.

**2**

Paint the short tube brown. Cut out a red circle from felt and glue it to the front of the tube.

**3**

Cut out two wings from brown felt and a beak from yellow felt.

**4**

Glue the wings and beak in place. Cut out some green circles of felt and add them and the eyes, as shown. Now make a cute penguin by using different colors!

# Spotted Snake

## You will need

Six short tubes

Paint

Ribbon

Red and blue felt

Two googly eyes

**1**

Paint six short tubes different bright colors.

**2**

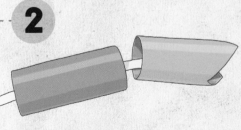

Cut off the corner of one tube, for the tail, as shown. Glue a piece of ribbon to the inside.

**3**

Thread on the remaining tubes. Glue the ribbon to the inside of the last tube.

**4**

Flatten the last tube and glue the sides together to make a head. Add a strip of red felt for the tongue, some blue felt circles and a pair of googly eyes. Decorate your snake—it's ready to slither away!

# Butterfly

**This pretty butterfly will look great hanging from a window.**

## You will need

**One short tube**
**Paint**

**1**

Cut a short tube into six sections.

**2**

Paint four of them one color and the other two a contrasting color.

**3**

Squeeze the circles to make the tips pointed. Glue two circles together, to make a pair of wings. Use clothespins to hold the wings in place while they dry.

**4**

Glue the wings to the body.

**5**

Cut the remaining purple circle in half. Glue together to make antennae.

**6**

Glue the antennae in place. Add some string and hang your pretty butterfly in your room.

# Crab

**You will need**

**Two short tubes**
**Orange paint**
**Cardboard**
**Two googly eyes**

**1**

Paint a short tube orange. When dry, push the sides into the center, to create a curved top. Repeat at the other end.

**2**

For the legs, cut another short tube into six circles and paint orange.

**3**

Fold all the legs, as shown. Cut out two claws from the cardboard and paint them orange.

**4**

Glue the legs to the base of the crab's shell.

**5**

Paint some spots on the shell. Glue on the claws and a pair of googly eyes.

## Handy Hint

Always wash your brushes after use.

**47**

# Stripy Zebra

Did you know that zebras have black and white stripes to help them to hide in a herd and keep them safe from predators?

## You will need

**Five short tubes**
**Black and white paint**
**Googly eyes**
**Black cardstock**
**Blue felt**

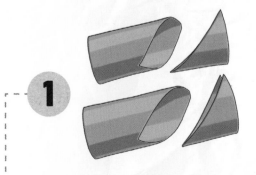

**1** Cut the corner off one end of two short tubes.

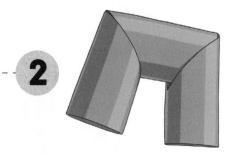

**2** Glue the tubes to either end of another tube, as shown. They should slide into each other a bit.

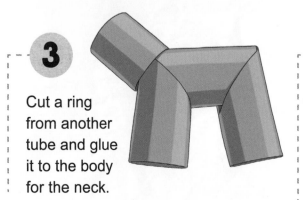

**3** Cut a ring from another tube and glue it to the body for the neck.

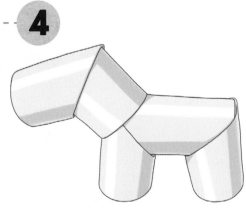

**4** Cut the corner off another tube and glue it to the neck. This is the head. Paint your zebra white. When dry, paint on some stripes.

### Handy Hint
The white paint must be completely dry before you add the stripes.

**5**

Cut a strip of black cardstock and glue it along the back of the neck for the mane. Cut a strip of black cardstock for the tail and glue it in place.

**6**

Cut out two ears from the cardstock as well as a circle to make the nose. Cut out some blue felt circles and add them to the googly eyes. Glue everything in place and paint on a smile.

STRIPY

# Kittens

## You will need

**Three short tubes**
**Paint**
**Cardboard**
**White and pink felt**
**Six googly eyes**

**1**

For each cat, push the sides of a short tube into the center, to create a curved top. Paint the tube.

**2**

Cut out a tail from cardboard and paint it to match the body. You could add some stripes to the tail and body. Glue the tail to the back of the short tube.

**3**

Cut out a dome shape from a piece of white felt, and glue it to the front of the body.

**4**

Glue on a small triangle of pink felt, for the nose, and a pair of eyes. Draw on some whiskers with a black pen.

**5**

Repeat steps 1 to 4 to make two more cute little kittens.

# Pompom

## You will need

**Four short tubes**
**Paint**
**Glitter**
**Ribbon**

**1** Paint four tubes inside and out, using a contrasting color on the insides.

**2** Fold the tubes in half and glue the middle together. Use a clothespin to hold in place until dry.

**3** Glue the four tubes together, into a circle. Use clothespins to hold in place until dry.

**4** Add glittery spots to decorate the pompom. Add some ribbon so you can hang up your pompom in your window to make a pretty decoration.

51

# Cool Castle

## You will need

**Four long tubes**
**Eight short tubes**
**Blue and purple paint**
**Thick green cardstock**
**Purple and gray cardstock**

**1**

Paint all of the tubes. Cut and assemble them to make a castle, as shown.

**2**

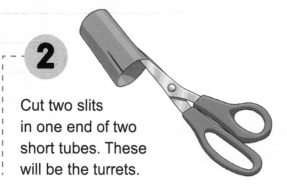

Cut two slits in one end of two short tubes. These will be the turrets.

**3**

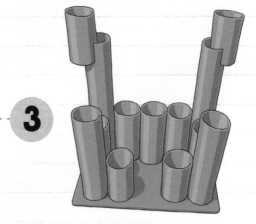

Slide the turrets over the towers. Glue all the tubes to a piece of thick green cardstock.

**4**

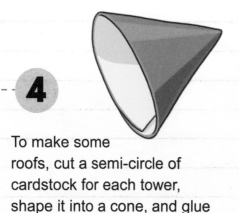

To make some roofs, cut a semi-circle of cardstock for each tower, shape it into a cone, and glue it in place. Paint the roofs.

**5**

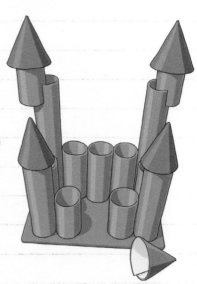

Glue the roofs in place.

**6**

Cut a long strip of purple cardstock
—use scrapbooking scissors,
if you have some. Cut along
one edge of the strip.

**7**

Glue the
strip to
the tops
of the walls.

**8**

Cut out windows from
the gray cardstock and
glue them onto your
fabulous castle.

**Handy Hint**

If you don't have
the right color
cardstock, you could
use white cardstock
and paint it a color
you choose.

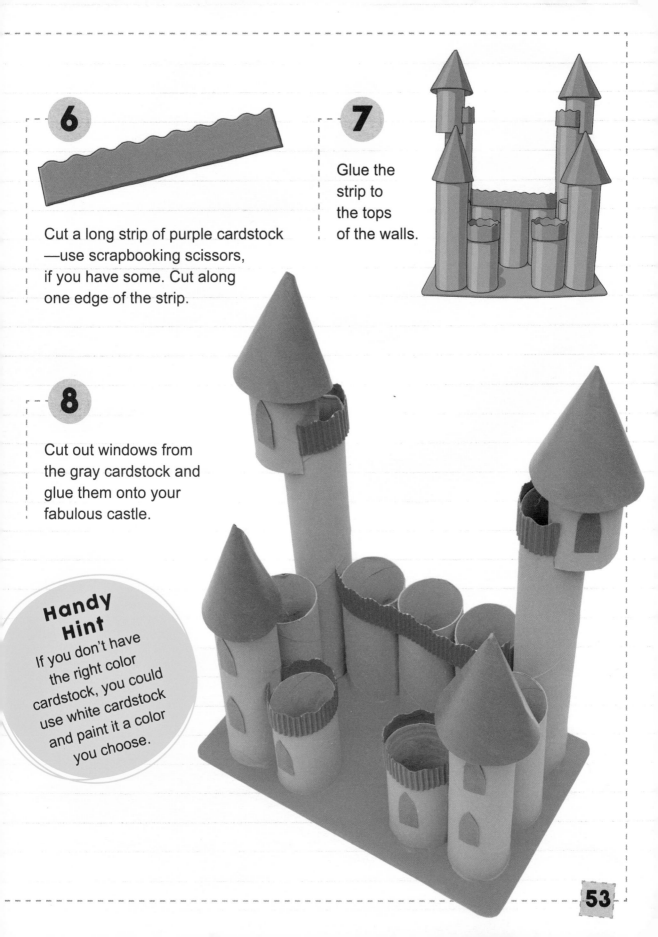

# Snappy Croc

Snap, snap, snap! This bright green crocodile friend is cute as can be but don't stand too close, or you'll become its snack!

## You will need

Six short tubes

Green, pink, and yellow paint

Cardboard

White and pink felt

Two googly eyes

**1**

Make a spike by flattening the end of a short tube. Cut off the top corners and glue the sides together.

**2**

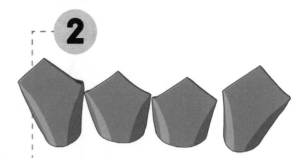

Make another spike of the same height. Make two more spikes, but slightly shorter. Paint them all green.

**3**

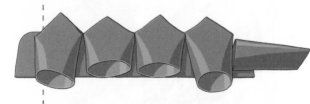

Flatten the top of another tube, glue the sides together, and paint it green. This will be the tail. Cut two wedge-shaped lengths of cardboard, and paint green. Glue the spikes and the tail onto the cardboard, as shown. Make sure the two longer spikes extend below the bottom of the cardboard. These will be legs. Glue the other piece of cardboard to the opposite side.

**4**

Cut another short tube diagonally, from top to bottom. Glue together the thick parts to create an open mouth. Paint green on the outside and then dark pink on the inside.

**5**

Glue the head onto the body.

**6**

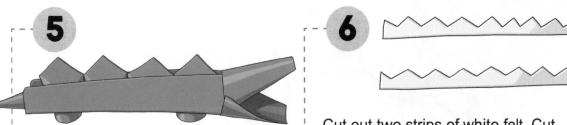

Cut out two strips of white felt. Cut Vs along one edge to make teeth.

**7**

Glue the strips of felt along the inside of the mouth.

**8**

Paint on spots and add pink felt circles to the pair of googly eyes. Snap, snap, your croc is ready!

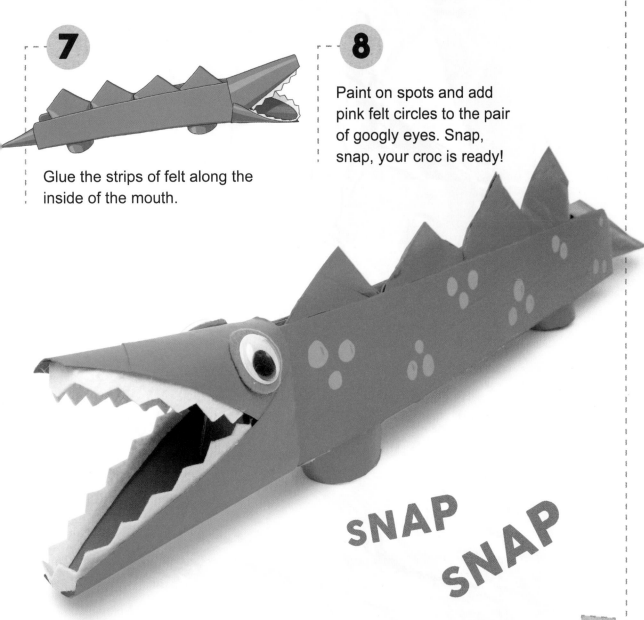

SNAP SNAP

# Pirate Pins

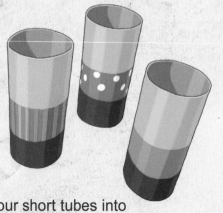

## You will need

**Five short tubes**

**Paint, including pink and black**

**Felt**

**Paper**

**1**

Divide your short tubes into three sections. Paint the tops pink, the middles a bright color and the bottoms black. Add spots or stripes to the middles.

**2**

Cut out five large triangles of felt.

**3**

Wrap the long side of one triangle of felt around the pink end of one tube, and glue into position.

**4**

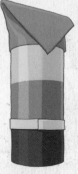

Fold down the tip of the triangle and glue. Repeat steps 3 and 4 on the other tubes.

**5**

Draw some features on each pirate. Scrunch up some paper, to make balls, then see how many pins you can bowl over!

# Racing Cars

**1**

To make the body of each car, use a pencil to make a hole for your scissors to cut a flap, as shown. Fold the flap backward. Paint the body.

**2**

Cut out four wheels from cardboard and paint black with a white middle.

**3**

Use a pencil to make a hole in the middle of each wheel. Place the wheels against the car and make holes with the pencil again.

**4**

Use metal fasteners to attach the wheels to the car.

**5**

Add a number and sporty stripes. Repeat the steps to make two more cars.

57

# Dinosaur Desk Bins

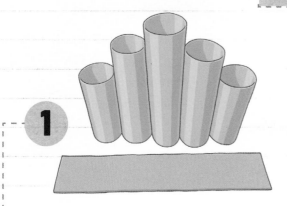

**1**

Cut some of the tubes so that you have one long one, two shorter ones, and two even shorter ones. Paint them and line them up, as shown. Glue them to cardboard that is slightly longer than the row of tubes.

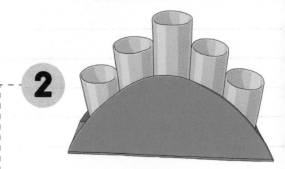

**2**

Cut out two semi-circles of cardboard. Paint them a contrasting color. Glue them to either side of the row of tubes.

**3**

Flatten the top of another tube, glue the sides together, and paint it the same color as the cardboard in step 2. This will be the tail.

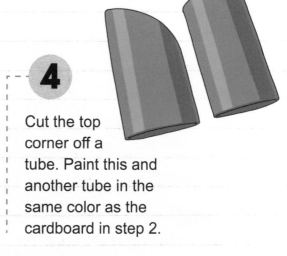

**4**

Cut the top corner off a tube. Paint this and another tube in the same color as the cardboard in step 2.

**5**

Glue the tubes together, for the head.

**6**

Glue the head and tail in place.

**7**

Paint on some spots and a smile. Add some felt circles and the eyes. Your happy dinosaur is ready to help you tidy your desk!

DINO BINS

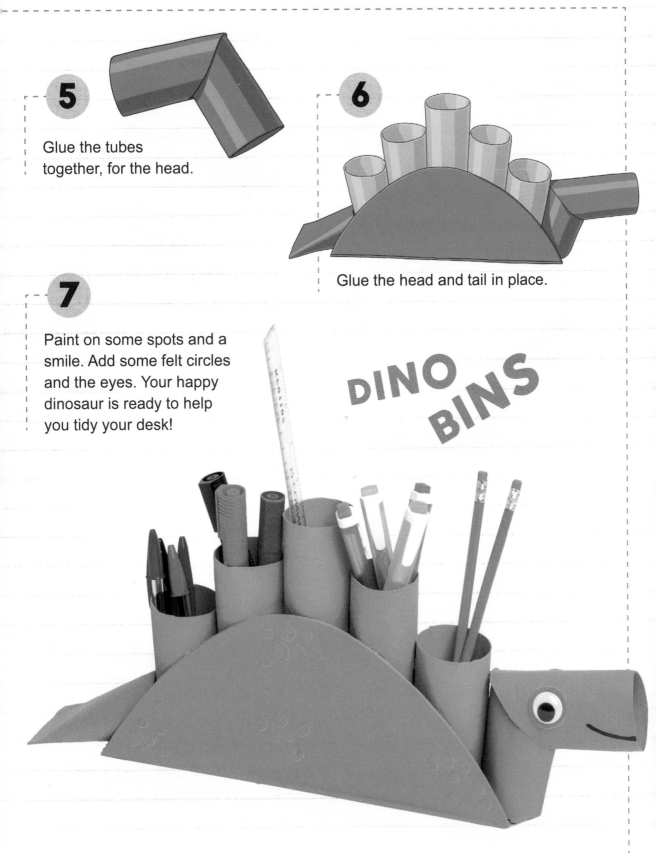

# Bunny Ears

**1**

Cut off the tops of the two cardboard tubes to leave a curved edge.

**2**

Glue the top sides together. Hold in place with clothespins until dry.

**3**

Paint the ears gray with a pink middle.

**4**

Use a pencil to make holes in both sides of each ear.

**5**

Thread a piece of elastic string through the holes and tie a knot in the end. Hippety-hop, your ears are ready to wear!

# Rocket

 **1**

Paint a short tube in a pretty, bright color.

**2**

Cut out three pieces of cardboard to make the legs and paint them.

 **3**

Cut out a semi-circle from cardstock and shape it into a cone.

5...4...3...
2...1...

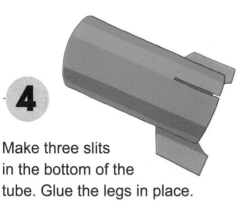

**4**

Make three slits in the bottom of the tube. Glue the legs in place.

 **5**

Glue on the cone. Add a window made from shiny cardstock and some details. Get ready for lift-off!

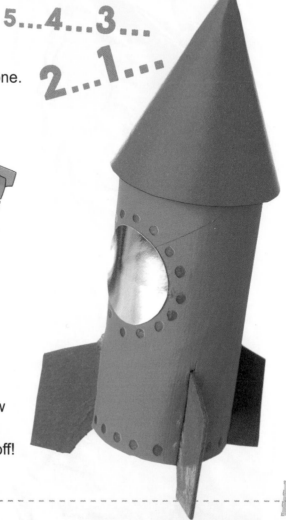

# Flamingo

Make this gorgeous pink flamingo and stand it proudly in your bathroom—but well away from the bathtub!

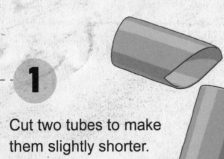

**1**

Cut two tubes to make them slightly shorter. Cut the top corner off one of the tubes, to make it angled.

**2**

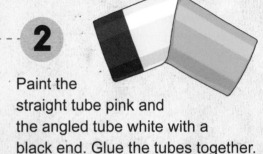

Paint the straight tube pink and the angled tube white with a black end. Glue the tubes together.

**3**

Paint another tube pink. Cut a slot in both pieces, as shown.

**4**

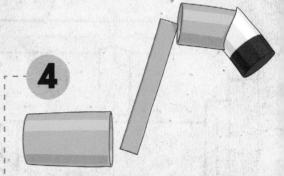

Paint a long strip of cardboard pink. Glue the cardboard into the two slots, at an angle, as shown.

**5**

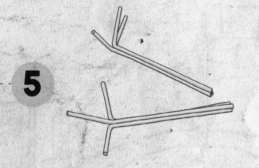

To make each leg, glue together the long parts of three bendy straws. Bend the short ends.

**6**

Use a pencil to make two holes in the bottom of the body.

**7**

Cut out two webbed feet from cardboard, and paint yellow. Cut out a tail from cardboard and paint pink.

**8**

Glue the webbed feet under the short pieces of straw. Insert the straws into the holes you made in the body. Glue to hold in position.

**9**

Cut a slot into the end of the body and slot the tail in place. Glue on some blue felt and googly eyes to complete the flamingo.

**Handy Hint**

To make eyes really stand out, use contrasting colors for your felt.

# Pretty Parrot

Tropical birds are some of the prettiest creatures on Earth. Why not make this fun parrot and perch?

**1**

Slightly flatten a long tube. Paint it red. Cut the top into a curved shape, as shown. Shape the bottom, as shown.

**2**

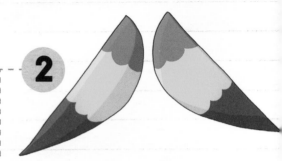

Cut out a pair of wings from cardboard and paint them with bands of color.

**3**

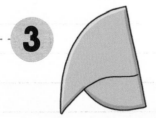

Cut out a beak from cardboard and paint it. Glue the beak to the inside of the tube top. Glue the two sides of the tube top together, so the beak is sandwiched in the middle.

**4**

Cut out two circles of white cardstock and glue to either side of the head. Glue on blue felt circles and googly eyes.

**5**

Glue the wings to the body, folding them out slightly.

**6**

Cut a narrow strip of cardstock and glue it to the underside of the body.

**7**

To make the perch, cut a dip in one end of another short tube and glue another tube onto it. Paint brown.

SQUAWK!

**8**

Glue the parrot onto its perch —who's a pretty boy, then?

# Tree Shelf

Bring the outside indoors with this fun tree shelf. You can also keep pencils and pens inside it.

**1**

Paint the outsides of ten tubes green. Paint the insides contrasting colors.

**2**

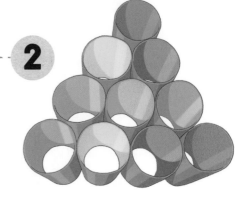

Glue the tubes together, to make a triangle.

**3**

Paint two more tubes brown and glue the sides together. Glue them to the base of your triangle.

**4**

You can make this tree as large as you like. Why not create an advent calendar and put little gifts in each tube?

# Reindeer Finger Puppet

**1**

Paint a short tube brown.

**2**

Cut out two antlers and two ears from cardboard and paint.

**3**

Glue the antlers to the inside of the tube. Flatten the top of the tube and glue to hold the sides together. Keep in place with clothespins.

**4**

Cut out a dome from cardboard.

**5**

Glue the dome to the front and the ears to the top of the head. Add some googly eyes and a red felt nose. Rudolf is ready!

# Peacock

**Proud as a peacock? You will be when you have made this dazzling creature.**

## You will need

**Nine short tubes**

**Paint, including blue and green-blue**

**Cardboard**

**Yellow cardstock**

**Two googly eyes**

**1**

Flatten and paint blue the tops of eight short tubes. Glue one end of each tube together. Use clothespins to hold in place until dry.

**2**

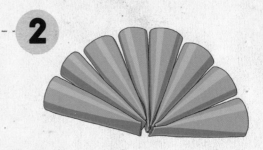

Glue the tubes together to form a tail, as shown.

**3**

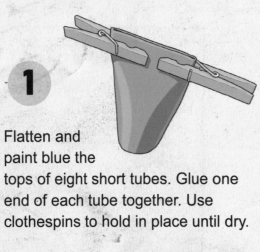

Cut a section off another tube and glue it to the bottom of the tail. Paint it blue.

**4**

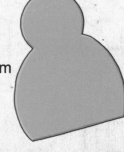

Cut a body from the cardboard and paint it green-blue.

**5**

Glue the body to the tail.

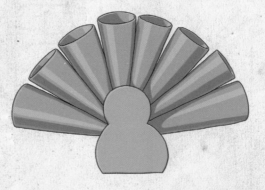

**6**

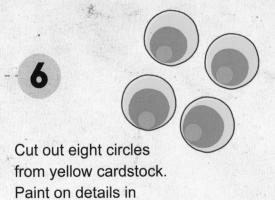

Cut out eight circles
from yellow cardstock.
Paint on details in
whatever colors you like.

**7**

Glue the circles
onto the tail.

**8**

Cut a triangle from yellow cardstock for
the beak. Glue on a pair of googly eyes
and your peacock is ready to parade!

# Plane

Zoom, zoom! Up, up and away! Take to the skies with this spectacular flying machine.

**1** For the body, paint a short tube orange.

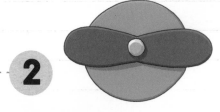

**2** From cardboard cut a circle to fit the top of the short tube. Paint the circle orange. Then cut a propeller from blue cardstock. Use a metal fastener to attach the propeller to the circle, as shown.

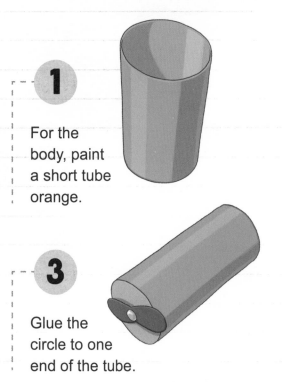

**3** Glue the circle to one end of the tube.

**4** Cut out two rectangles from cardboard, for the wings. Cut out three smaller rectangles, each with one curved corner, from cardboard. Paint all the pieces blue.

**5** Glue the body to one of the wings.

**6** Glue the other wing onto the body.

**7** Make three slits in the end of the tube. Slot the tail parts into position.

**8** Glue the tail parts in place. Cut four pieces of straw to fit between the wings, glue in place.

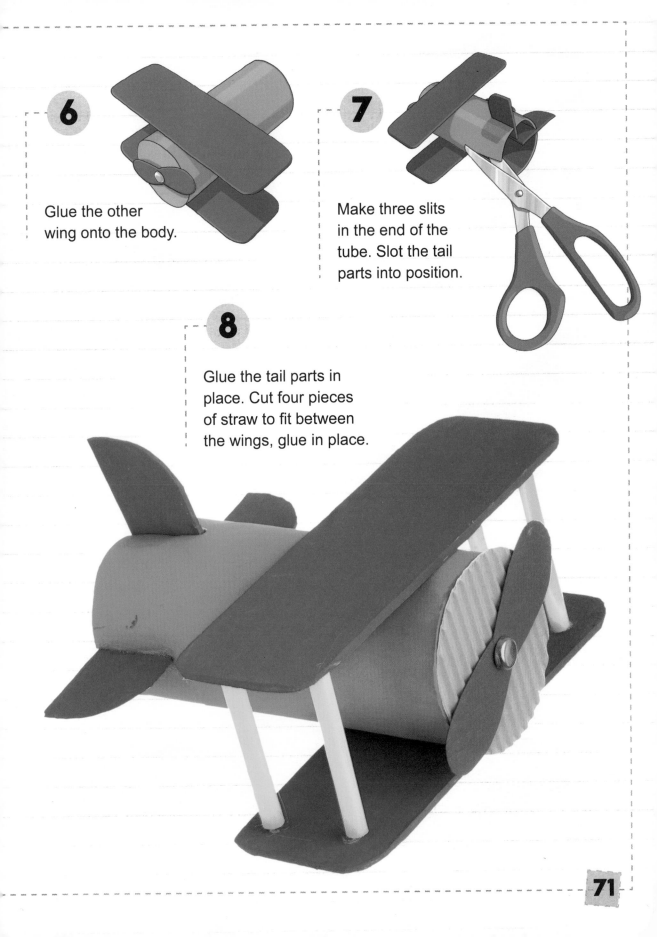

# Sheep

**1** Cut a section off each long tube and glue them together. Glue two sets of two shorter tubes together.

## You will need

**Three long tubes**

**Five short tubes**

**White, gray and black paint**

**Cardboard**

**Cardstock**

**Pink and green felt**

**Googly eyes**

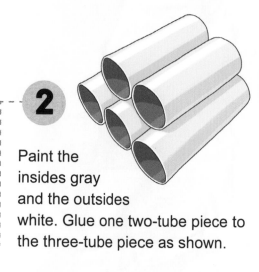

**2** Paint the insides gray and the outsides white. Glue one two-tube piece to the three-tube piece as shown.

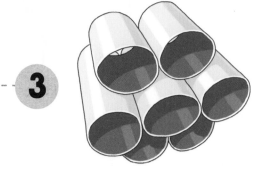

**3** Glue the other two-tube piece to the bottom of the three-tube piece, as shown.

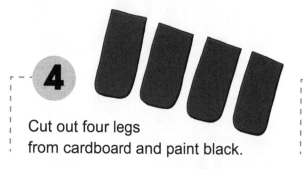

**4** Cut out four legs from cardboard and paint black.

**5** Glue the legs in place.

**6**

Flatten the top of a tube and cut a curved top. Glue the top together.

**7**

Cut out a pair of ears from cardstock and glue them to the head. Paint them all black.

**8**

Glue the head to the front of the body. Add a pink felt nose, some green felt circles, and some googly eyes. Your sheep is ready for the pasture!

BAAA

BAAA

# Cute Snail

There is nothing snail-paced about the speed at which you can make this cute little critter. Ready, steady, GO!

**1**

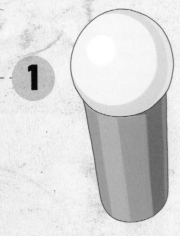

To make the head and body, glue a foam ball to one end of a tube.

**2**

Flatten the other end of the short tube and glue the sides together. Paint the body and head a pale color.

**3**

To make a shell, cut another tube into a spiral, following the line that runs around the tube.

**4**

Paint both sides. Roll one end and glue to the inside, as shown. Hold in place with a clothespin.

**5**

Curl the tube into a loose circle. Glue the other end to the outside of the tube. Use a clothespin to hold it in place until dry.

**6**

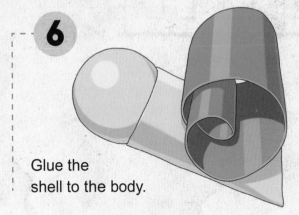

Glue the shell to the body.

**7**

Use a pencil to make two holes in the top of the head. Insert two short pieces of straw and glue into position. Add some felt circles and googly eyes. How fast can it go?

# Snowman

**Brrr! Is it cold outside? Stay inside and make this cute snowman!**

**1**

Leave two of the short tubes their full size, cut one slightly shorter than the first two, and another one even shorter. Paint them all white.

**2**

Glue the two full tubes together. Glue the slightly shorter tube on top, as shown.

**3**

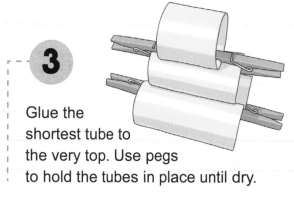

Glue the shortest tube to the very top. Use pegs to hold the tubes in place until dry.

**4**

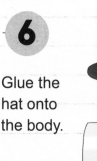

Cut a circle from cardboard just wider than a short tube. Paint that and the leftover shortest piece black.

**5**

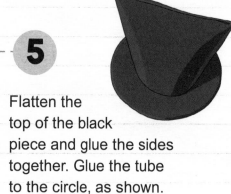

Flatten the top of the black piece and glue the sides together. Glue the tube to the circle, as shown.

**6**

Glue the hat onto the body.

**7**

Make a pair of twig arms from chenille stems, and glue them to the snowman. Make a small cone from orange cardstock for its nose, and glue it in place.

**8**

Cut a strip of felt and glue it around the neck, for a scarf. Draw on some eyes and a smile. Why not make a whole family of cute snowpeople?

## Handy Hint

To make a cone, cut a quarter-circle and roll it around so that the straight edges meet.

# Santa

**It's Christmas! Just don't put this Santa up your chimney!**

## You will need

**One long tube**
**Red, pink, and black paint**
**White cardstock**
**One white pompom**
**One red pompom**
**Two googly eyes**

**1**

Fold over the top of a long tube. Glue to hold it in place.

**2**

Paint the top and middle parts red.

**3**

Paint a pink band between the red parts. Paint the bottom black.

**4**

Use scrapbook scissors to cut a beard and two narrow strips of white cardstock, for a fur trim.

**5**

Glue the beard and fur trims to the body.

HO HO HO

**6**

Add some googly eyes, a red pompom for the nose, and a white pompom to the hat. Don't forget rosy cheeks and a smile before you put the finished Santa on your Christmas tree.

Quarto is the authority on a wide range of topics.

Quarto educates, entertains and enriches the lives of
our readers—enthusiasts and lovers of hands-on living.

www.quartoknows.com

Publisher: Maxime Boucknooghe
Editorial Director: Victoria Garrard
Art Director: Miranda Snow
Editors: Sophie Hallam, Sarah Eason and Jennifer Sanderson
Designer: Paul Myerscough
Photographer: Michael Wicks
Illustrator: Tom Connell
With thanks to our wonderful models Islah, Ethan, and Ania.

First published in the United States in 2016
by QEB Publishing, Inc.
Part of The Quarto Group
6 Orchard
Lake Forest, CA 92630

A CIP record for this book is available from the Library of Congress.

ISBN  978 1 68297 005 8